bats

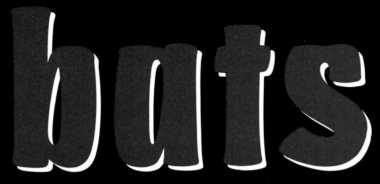

bats

Mysterious Flyers
of the Night

by Dee Stuart
A Carolrhoda Nature Watch Book

Carolrhoda Books, Inc./Minneapolis

The author wishes to thank Dr. Merlin Tuttle, Tracey Tarlton, and Bert Grantges for their assistance in the preparation of this book.

Photo credits

All photographs © Merlin D. Tuttle, Bat Conservation International, except p. 41, © Jerry Hennen.

This book is available in two editions:
Library binding by Carolrhoda Books, Inc.
Soft cover by First Avenue Editions
c/o The Lerner Group
241 First Avenue North, Minneapolis, MN 55401

LIBRARY OF CONGRESS CATALOGING-IN-PUBLICATION DATA

Stuart, Dee.
  Bats : mysterious flyers of the night / by Dee Stuart.
    p.   cm.
  "A Carolrhoda nature watch book."
  Includes index.
  ISBN 0-87614-814-3 (lib. bdg.)
  ISBN 0-87614-631-0 (pbk.)
  1. Bats—Juvenile literature. [1. Bats.] I. Title.
QL737.C5S77   1994
599.4—dc20   93-34304
                                                    CIP
                                                     AC

Manufactured in the United States of America
1 2 3 4 5 6 – P/JR – 9 98 97 96 95 94

CONTENTS

Millions of Mexican free-tailed bats (Tadarida brasilensis) *emerging from Bracken Cave in Texas*

MISUNDERSTOOD

As dusk falls over the rolling Texas hill country, white-tailed deer frisk among green mountain cedar, mesquite, and scrub pine. An armadillo trundles through tall grasses, and wild turkeys forage for food. Suddenly the deer lift their heads, listening, watchful, alert. What appears to be a huge column of smoke rises from the oval opening of a nearby cave and curls upward, darkening the soft blue twilight sky. For more than two hours, the lengthening column emerges, visible for miles as it stretches over the surrounding countryside.

But the enormous swirling gray column silhouetted against the sky is not smoke. The spectacular sight is a group of more than twenty million Mexican free-tailed bats leaving their roost in Bracken Cave for a night of insect hunting.

If you are like many people, hearing the word "bat," you shudder or shiver with fear and dislike. "Bats," you may say. "Ugh!" Somewhere, you've heard that bats attack people, tangle in your hair, bite, and carry rabies. Unfortunately, many myths and misconceptions, or wrong ideas, about bats have been told and retold throughout the ages. As a result, bats are one of nature's most unfairly accused and misunderstood creatures.

Bats are shy, gentle animals. They don't tangle in your hair; in fact, they try to avoid humans. They rarely become aggressive even when they're sick, so if you just leave them alone, there is nothing to fear.

Big brown bats (Eptesicus fuscus) *roosting under a wooden bridge*

A common vampire bat (Desmodus rotundus)

The most feared bat of all, the vampire bat, is really quite sociable. A female vampire bat will adopt orphaned babies. And if a bat in trouble emits sounds of distress, other bats flock to its aid. A vampire bat with a full stomach will give blood to a neighbor who has failed to find food. Vampires are the only bats that feed on warm blooded animals. They never pounce on people and rarely bite humans. Far from being huge and menacing, most vampire bats weigh less than 2 ounces (50 grams), have a small wingspan, and are timid and sensitive. Finally, despite what you may read in books or see in movies, vampire bats are found only in Latin America.

A distinctive-looking wrinkle-faced bat (Centurio senex)

Along with the misconception that most bats are blood-sucking vampires is the notion that all bats carry disease. The truth is that some bats get sick, just as other animals do. An occasional bat can develop rabies. But unlike most other mammals, even rabid bats rarely attack. In the last fifty years, fewer than twenty people have died from bat bites—fewer deaths than occur each year from bee stings or dog attacks.

Have you heard the saying "blind as a bat"? The fact is, bats are not blind, and most bats see quite well.

Sometimes people say that someone is "batty" or has "bats in the belfry," meaning that person is "crazy." But bat handlers know from experience that bats are intelligent and quick to learn. Bats learn to recognize their handlers and to come when called. Many are affectionate little creatures who may show their fondness by licking your hand or cheek. Some bats are curious and playful and can be taught to perform tricks. Every one has a distinct personality.

ALL ABOUT BATS

There are almost one thousand species, or kinds, of bats. They are classified as **mammals** because they give birth to live offspring and nurse their newborn babies, just as cats, dogs, monkeys, and other mammals do. But one remarkable characteristic sets bats apart from all other mammals. Bats can fly. No other mammal can perform this astonishing feat. Flying squirrels and lemurs can glide downward from a high perch, so they appear to fly. But their "wings" are really only flaps of skin stretched between their front and back legs.

Because bats are unique, scientists classify them in a special order, or group, all their own called Chiroptera (ky-RAHP-tuh-ruh). This term comes from two Greek words, *chiro*, meaning "hand," and *ptera,* meaning "wing." The order Chiroptera is divided into two suborders, Megachiroptera and Microchiroptera.

Megachiroptera, or megabats, include nearly two hundred species and live in tropical regions: Asia, Australia, Africa, and the islands of the Pacific and Indian oceans. Microbats live worldwide, except for Antarctica and most of the arctic region. Most of the world's bats are microbats. No matter where you live, chances are, bats are living in your neighborhood.

You may think that when you've seen one bat you've seen them all. But bat species differ greatly in size and appearance. Most bats are small, weighing less than 2 ounces (50 grams). The smallest microbat, the bumblebee bat or Kitti's hognose bat, which is found in Thailand, is the size of a jellybean and weighs about 2 grams, less than a penny weighs. Flying foxes, the giants of the bat world, weigh up to 3 or 4 pounds (1½-2 kg), with wingspans of up to 6 feet (1.8 m).

Bats' furry coats come in an amazing variety of colors and textures. Some range from soft, velvety browns to rich, dark browns, and shades of silvery gray to jet black. Others sport more exotic hues. The hoary bat, one of America's largest and most handsome bats, boasts long, thick, white-tipped fur that gives it a frosted (or ''hoary'') appearance. It also has partly orange wings and black-edged yellow ears. The spotted bat has long, jet-black fur with three white spots on its back, and huge, pink, rabbit-like ears that are almost as long as its body. Some bats have smooth, satiny coats. There is even one naked bat, the hairless bat of southeast Asia.

One reason for bats' varied appearances is that nature has given them protective coloring, a camouflage, or disguise, that enables them to blend with their natural surroundings and avoid being seen by enemies. Bats with speckled or mottled fur blend with bark or rock. Orange, yellow, and red bats may blend with ripening fruit. Bats with bright spots often look like dappling sunlight sifting through the trees. A red bat snoozing as it hangs by one foot from a twig looks just like a dead leaf. You have to look twice to be sure it's really there.

A hoary bat (Lasiurus cinereus)

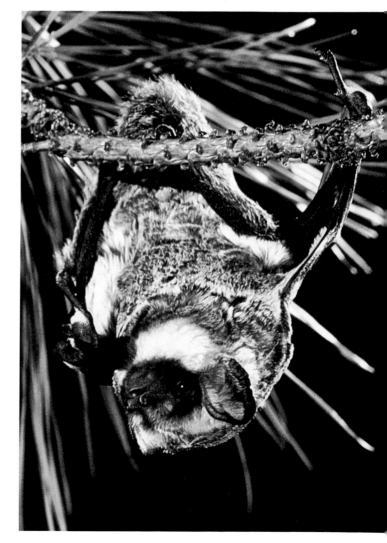

Top: *This false vampire bat* (Vampyrum spectrum) *is a member of the spear-nosed bat family.* Bottom: *Townsend's big-eared bat* (Plecotus townsendii) *has large, distinctive ears.*

In addition to their various colorings, you can tell one bat from another by their noses. Bats' noses vary far more than human noses. Some bats have plain, unremarkable noses. Others may be lump-nosed, spear-nosed, dog-nosed, or lcaf-nosed. Leaf-nosed bats have strange, leaflike folds and flaps of skin around their noses that help them to produce sound, as you do when you hum. Other bats have long noses that enable them to plunge into the heart of a flower to sip the nectar deep inside. Another way you can tell one bat from another is by the shape of their ears. Bats' ear shapes, too, vary greatly.

Bat wings differ among different species. Bat wings consist of a double leathery **membrane,** a skin so thin you can almost see through it. The skin covers four long, bony fingers, like those of your hand, and one clawed thumb. The wings are attached to the hind legs at the ankles. When the bat folds its wings, they shrink or pucker up like an umbrella. This prevents loose, baggy skin from being damaged or getting in the way.

Wing shape determines each bat's flying style. Generally, bats with long, narrow wings, such as the free-tails, are swift fliers. Bats with relatively short, wide wings, such as those that eat nectar and pollen, are slow fliers. Wings also help bats keep cool. When a bat flies, its body heat rises. As the heated blood flows through the wings, the air cools the blood.

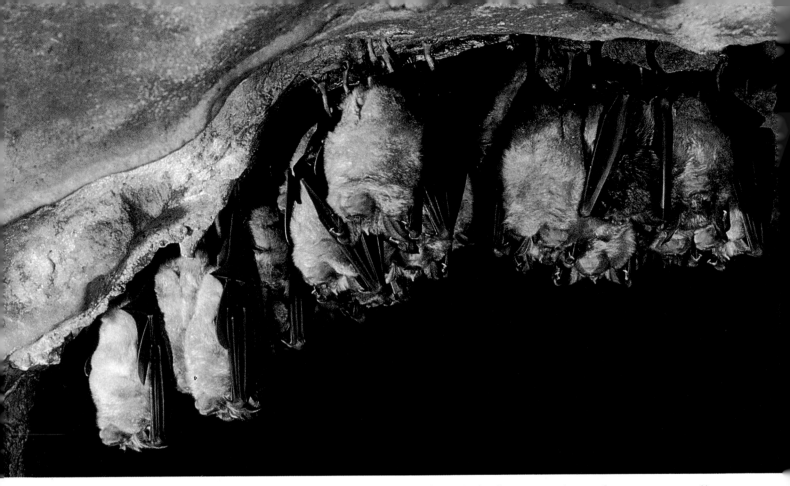

Greater horseshoe bats (Rhinolophus ferrumequinum) *using their fingers to hang from a cave wall*

Tails also help to identify each species. Some bat tails are entirely enclosed in the interfemoral (meaning "between the leg bones") membrane. Some tails jut a short distance beyond it; others are long and mostly free of the membrane. There are also tailless bats.

Some scientists think the tail acts as a rudder to aid in the direction of the bat's flight. Flying style varies greatly with individual species. There are acrobatic fliers that dart, swoop, and swerve in a fast, zig-zag pattern. A few bat species can glide, and others can hover for a short time.

Most bats move very little other than flight because their hind feet aren't built for walking upright. Bats do fold their wings and can use their hind feet, wrists, and thumbs to crawl or climb. They also use their thumbs to hang on ceilings and walls or to handle food. Many can move forward and backward. Vampire bats leap, jump, hop, and even perform somersaults.

The lesser long-nosed bat (Leptonycteris curasoae) *has a tail that extends a short distance beyond its* interfemoral membrane.

BATS IN THE DARK

One unique characteristic of bats once baffled scientists and for hundreds of years remained a mystery. This is their amazing ability to find their way about in the dark. How do bats find the tasty insects they need to eat to survive? How do they keep from stumbling about, bumping into obstacles? Can they really "see" in the dark?

In the late 1700s, Lazzaro Spallanzani, an Italian scientist, became curious about how bats moved about in darkness. At first he thought they had superior vision. To test his theory, he placed a small, light-proof hood over the heads of bats to block their vision, then released them in a darkened room. Of course the bats bumped into objects, and Spallanzani thought he had proved his theory. Just to be sure, he tried placing transparent hoods over the bats' heads. To his dismay, the bats were unable to fly without crashing into obstacles.

To settle the matter of eyesight being essential, Spallanzani surgically blinded some bats. He was astonished to discover that the blinded bats could avoid obstacles as well as sighted bats. In further experiments, he placed two groups of bats—one blinded, one sighted, in a cave for several days. When he recaptured the bats, he found that both groups had the same amount of food in their stomachs. He then concluded that bats did not rely on eyesight to fly in the dark, but relied instead on a "sixth sense."

Bats' ability to find prey in the dark puzzled scientists for many years.

In 1798, Louis Jurine, a Swiss surgeon, continued Spallanzani's experiments by plugging the ears of bats with wax. He found that these bats were unable to avoid obstacles. Spallanzani, going a step further, inserted a small brass tube into bats' ears. When he plugged the tubes, the bats crashed into obstacles. When the tubes were unplugged, the bats flew about like normal bats. From these remarkable experiments, Spallanzani and Jurine concluded that hearing was important in bats' ability to find their way in darkness. But neither scientist could explain his findings. For more than one hundred years, their conclusions were ignored.

It was not until 1938 that a break-through occurred. Professor G. W. Pierce, a Harvard physicist, developed a device for detecting **ultrasonic** sounds, or sounds above the hearing range of the human ear. At the same time, a Harvard biology student named Donald Griffin was studying bat biology. He asked Professor Pierce if he could use his sonic detector to listen to his bats. When Griffin held the cage full of bats up to the detector, the device gave out a commotion of loud squeaks and cries that left no doubt that his bats were producing high frequency sounds. Griffin concluded that bats "see" with their ears.

The spotted bat (Euderma maculatum), *above, produces noises that humans can hear when it echolocates. Most megabats, including Franquet's flying fox* (Epomops franqueti), *below, cannot echolocate.*

We now know that bats are equipped with built-in **sonar**, a system that enables them to detect the presence of distant or unseen objects by using sound. When a bat takes to the air, it produces a series of ultrasonic squeaks and clicks. When these sounds strike an object, they bounce back to the bat's ears like an echo. By judging the length of time between echoes, bats can tell where their prey is and how fast it is moving. They can also tell something about the size or kind of object that has caught their attention. The ability to use echoes to locate food or other objects is called **echolocation** (eh-koh-loh-KAY-shun).

Sounds are produced in the bat's voice-box, or larynx. Most bats send out signals from their mouths, but others emit sounds through their noses. All microbats have the ability to echolocate. Some bats, including the spotted bat and the Martienssen's free-tailed bat, emit calls that humans can hear. Megabats cannot echolocate, except for Rousettus fruit bats, which produce clicks with the backs of their tongues. No two sonars are the same among the nearly one thousand bat species.

The Egyptian rousette (Rousettus aegypticus) is one of the few megabats that can echolocate.

How does the bat know which of the objects it finds by echolocation are to be eaten? Do echoes tell the bat what is food and what isn't? How does it know which objects are dangers or obstacles to be avoided? These are some of the many mysteries about bat behavior still to be solved.

BATS, BATS EVERYWHERE

Bats have long lives. Their average life span is about fifteen years, though some may live more than thirty years. They are the longest-lived mammals on earth for their size. Most small mammals, such as shrews and mice, live only a year or two.

Most scientists believe that millions of years ago, bats had only webbed skin between their arms and legs. As time passed, bats' webbed skin developed into wings that enabled them to fly. This ability proved useful in their pursuit of food. Bats were originally daytime insect eaters, but the more curious and adventurous among them eventually discovered a new food source—a whole cafeteria of insects, flying around in the twilight. As time passed, **insectivorous** (in-sek-TIHV-uh-ruhs), or insect-eating, bats found that insect-hunting was best at nighttime. So they roosted during the day and hunted for food at night. They probably developed their ability to echolocate because of the large numbers of insects that were available at night. Eventually they became **nocturnal** animals, active at night.

Aided by their development of flight and echolocation, and their ability to **adapt,** or change in order to survive, bats have become the second largest order of mammals, outnumbered only by rodents.

As they developed over the centuries, bats often faced stiff competition with other animal species for food, and sometimes droughts or freezes killed off their food supply. When they couldn't find foods they liked, bats adapted by eating foods that were available. At the same time, by changing their diets, they cut down competition with other species. Although most bat species are still insectivorous, many adapted to new opportunities and began eating fruits, nectar, fish, and small animals.

Below: *A Gambian epauletted bat* (Epomophorus gambianus) *feeding on a mango.* Right: *A pallid bat* (Antrozous pallidus) *feasting on a scorpion, more typical bat food*

Bats have succeeded in making their way in the world not only because of the variety and the availability of their food sources, but also because of the special features each species has developed to find and consume food. Once bats developed the ability to fly, they evolved like gangbusters. Eyes, ears, noses, mouths, wings, and tails all gradually changed to suit bats' feeding habits. In fact, these small creatures are an extraordinary example of how structure and appearance can adapt to a changing environment.

For example, some bats live on nectar and pollen. If you visit desert areas of Arizona or the Sonora Desert in Mexico, you may see night-flying, long-nosed bats winging through the moon-dark sky to visit the flowers of the cardon, saguaro, and organ-pipe cactuses.

The bat thrusts its long nose inside the night-blooming flower. Nectar droplets cling to the tip of the bat's enormously long tongue, which is sometimes nearly half as long as its owner and enables it to gather nectar. When the nectar-sipper withdraws, its head is covered with pollen. The bat then transfers the pollen to the next flower it visits for a midnight meal.

A lesser long-nosed bat eating the fruit of a saguaro cactus

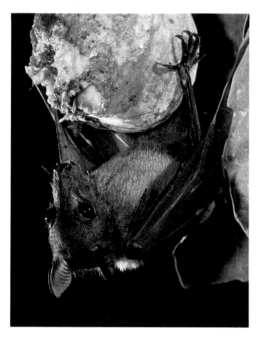

Right: *A lesser long-nosed bat pollinating an agave plant.* Below: *Megabats, such as this Angola fruit bat* (Rousettus angolensis), *usually eat fruit.*

BAT FOOD

You may think that sweet, syrupy nectar is not much of a meal, but the powdery pollen is highly nutritious and furnishes the protein that bats need. If cactuses don't provide enough food for hungry customers, nectar-eating or **nectivorous** (nek-TIHV-uh-ruhs) bats supplement their diets with visits to the agave plant, an especially fine provider of nectar and pollen. After eating, they lick the pollen from their faces.

Megabats feed mostly on fruit, as do some microbats. Since almost all megabats lack the ability to echolocate, they find meals mainly by smell and their excellent vision. Their large eyes are ten times as sensitive as those of humans. Their teeth are broad and flat for ease in mashing their food. Ridges across the roof of the mouth serve as a washboard as the bat's tongue presses the fruit against it and sucks out the juices. Some bats spit out any part of the fruit that they can't crush.

A common vampire bat laps blood from a chicken's foot.

Fish-eating bats, found in South and Central America as well as parts of Asia, swoop over the water and snatch up their prey with long, sharp claws on their hind feet. They raise the fish to their mouth and, with sharp teeth, crunch it into pieces that they store in cheek pouches to eat later. These bats also dine on insects. Frog-eating bats hunt their prey in forests from Mexico to southern Brazil. A few species of bats eat scorpions, birds, mice, and even other bats.

Vampire bats feed on the blood of birds and mammals, including cattle, pigs, and chickens. A vampire needs to drink about half its body weight every night (about a tablespoon of blood) and must feed for about twenty minutes to fill its stomach. Cautiously, it lands on the animal and makes a small cut with its teeth. It does not "suck" blood, but laps it from the wound with a funnel-like tongue.

Insectivorous bats feed on beetles, crickets, gnats, grasshoppers, moths, mosquitoes, mayflies, midges and other insects. A fast and skillful flier will scoop up a moth with one wing and devour it in midflight. Or it may sweep an insect into its tail or wing membrane, then take the prey into its mouth. If the insect is too large to eat in midflight, the bat may land on a perch to devour the soft, tasty body. Some bats, including the California leaf-nosed bats known as gleaners, pluck insects from the ground or from bushes.

Insectivorous bats have huge appetites. One small bat may devour up to six hundred moths, mosquitoes, and other insects in one hour. Can you guess how many insects twenty million bats can devour? When mothers are rearing young, they consume up to 500,000 pounds (225,000 kg) of insects each night.

A big brown bat eating a moth as it flies

MIGRATION

As summer fades, nights grow chilly and frost covers the hills. Insects die, and food is hard to find. The temperature falls to the low 50s. Winter is just around the corner. *How* they know is a mystery, but Mexican free-tailed bats know it is time to leave Bracken Cave. Time to **migrate** to their winter homes in Mexico and Central America—a journey of 800 to 1600 miles (1280-2560 km). As the bats emerge from the cave, millions of beating wings sound like the patter of rain on a rooftop. Swirling clockwise to gain altitude, the flock may climb to nearly 10,000 feet (3000 m) in the air.

Generally, bats cruise at a leisurely speed of 10 to 20 miles per hour (16-32 kph). Red bats soar up to 40 miles per hour (64 kph). Free-tails, even faster fliers, use tailwinds to travel at more than 60 miles per hour (96 kph) and can easily cover long distances. If you watch closely, you may see waves of free-tails and other bat species traveling with birds along the same flyways.

Not all bats head south of the border for the winter. The red bats, large hoary bats, and silver-haired bats that summer in trees and shrubs in the northern United States and Canada can't survive the harsh winter winds and bitter cold temperatures there, so they spend the winter in Georgia, South Carolina, Florida, and the Southwest. Fruit bats in the tropics migrate in large groups along with the seasons of ripening fruit.

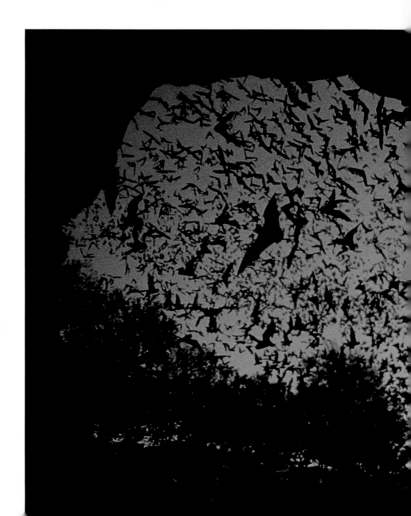

Right: Mexican free-tailed bats leaving Bracken Cave. Opposite page, top: A greater horseshoe bat hibernating alone; bottom: Gray bats (Myotis grisecens) hibernating in a cluster

Bats that **hibernate,** or spend the winter in a sleeplike state, must prepare for the long winter ahead. They do this by eating much more than they need during the warm, insect-filled days. In this way, they build up fat reserves that provide the energy they need to stay alive during the cold winter months. They also look for sites where the humidity and temperature remain constant and the temperature will not fall below freezing. Bats that live in warm or temperate climates often hibernate in caves or abandoned mines.

While hibernating, these plump little bats hang head down—some separately, some in **colonies,** or tightly packed clusters, on the walls and ceilings of their roosts. Some bats are loners. They like their own space and, with loud cries, will push and shove a neighbor who moves too close.

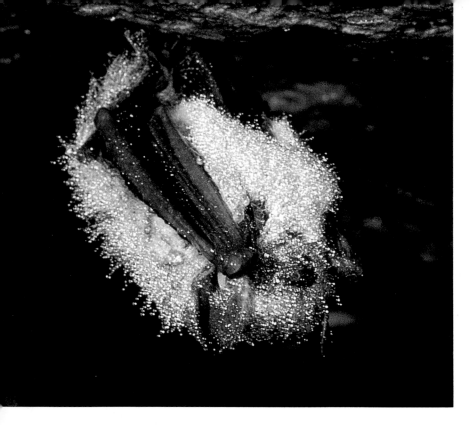

The drops of dew covering this eastern pipistrelle (Pipistrellus subflavus) show that its body temperature has dropped along with the temperature inside the cave.

Hibernating bats enter a very deep sleep, or **torpor.** This means that their body functions shut down so that they burn very little energy and need very little fat or "fuel" to survive. The bat's breathing slows from two hundred to about twenty-three breaths per minute, and its heartbeat drops from four hundred to below twenty-five beats per minute.

Now bats perform another remarkable feat. The bat's body temperature does not remain constant, as do humans and most other mammals. A bat's temperature adjusts to the surrounding temperature. This means that when the temperature drops, the bat allows its temperature to fall so that it doesn't need to use up stored fat to keep warm and stay alive.

Hibernation is a dangerous time in the bat's life because when it awakens from a deep sleep, it takes a long time to heat up. To do so, it shivers and shakes, and uses a lot of energy to bring its temperature up to normal. If anyone enters the cave and disturbs the bat while it is hibernating, it will burn up a huge amount of stored fat just waking up. The danger is that later it will run out of stored fat and will not have enough to stay alive through the rest of the winter.

Some bats rouse while hibernating, shuffle about to seek a better site, grab a bite to eat if possible, drink, and urinate, but only for a short time, not long enough to endanger their fat reserve. Little brown bats can survive up to 165 days without waking from hibernation. Large bats may hibernate for almost an entire year.

Bats that live in very warm climates neither migrate nor hibernate. They make their homes year-round in barns, church steeples, under the eaves of houses, in shadowy attics, crevices, hollow tree trunks, under loose bark, under bridges, or in storm sewers. Some bats, including some of the leaf-nosed bats of the Americas, make their own homes. They punch holes down the center of a banana leaf with their teeth. The leaf folds down over them like a tent, protecting them from the sun and rain.

These Honduran white bats (Ectophylla alba) *have made a tent for themselves from a leaf.*

For many years, scientists have been studying another mystery of bat behavior that remains unsolved to this day. How do migrating bats know when spring arrives and it's time to return to their summer homes? Some scientists think there is an internal clock in the bat's brain that alerts them to the season. Others think that using up the winter's supply of fat, or awareness of the longer hours of daylight, provides the clue that sends them flying homeward.

Whatever the reason, in early March and April, colonies of migrating bats head northward to roost in the same caves they occupied the previous summer. How do they find their way back to the same caves year after year? This is another feat of navigation that has long baffled students of bat behavior. Do bats, like pigeons, have a homing instinct? Studies have shown that bats transported 100 or more miles away from their normal roosts and then released will zoom straight back to the same site. So we know that bats are capable of "homing." Whether they return home by chance or by instinct is not yet understood. Some scientists think that bats recognize landmarks along the way. If this is true, what landmarks do bats look for to guide their way home? Others think that star patterns guide the night migrants through the dark skies.

NEW BATS

In spring, before beginning the long journey back to their summer home, Mexican free-tails and other migrating bats have mated. But unlike other female mammals, whose eggs are fertilized by male sperm cells during mating, the female bat stores the fertile male sperm in her **uterus** (a hollow organ in the female's body) until she emerges from hibernation. After she wings northward, where she has an abundant supply of food and a warm roost, the female bat **ovulates**, or produces an egg. One of the sperm she is carrying fertilizes this egg, and a young bat begins to develop.

Mexican free-tailed females ovulate in March, and babies are born in June. Other species, such as the little brown bat, mate in autumn. Fertilization occurs after hibernation, and youngsters are born in early June or July. This remarkable feat, delayed ovulation and fertilization, occurs among many bat species, but not among any other mammals. Most bear only one pup per year, although some tropical bats may give birth twice or more in a year.

Many species of pregnant bats travel to a maternal or nursery cave, where large numbers of other expectant females gather. Here they await the birth of their young. Males find separate bachelor quarters, sometimes miles away.

Most bats have only one baby, or pup, per year. But some species, including big brown bats, usually have twins, and red bats may have up to four offspring. The **gestation** (jeh-STAY-shun) period, the amount of time before the young are born, varies from species to species. Gestation is usually from forty to sixty days in small bats to as long as eight months in common vampire bats.

When birth begins, female bats cling to the ceiling with their feet, head down. Some mothers roosting on flat or level sites grasp the roosting place with thumbs and both hind feet, hammock-style. Other bats turn upside down (head up) to ease delivery. The baby then passes from the mother's birth canal and drops feet first into a cup or basket formed by her body, wings, and tail membrane. The process takes about fifteen to twenty minutes.

Left: *A Mexican free-tail giving birth in a nursery cave.* Right: *A red bat* (Lasiurus borealis) *mother with her twin pups*

A Gambian epauletted bat mother with her young

With a special set of milk teeth, the newborn grips the mother's nipple so that it's firmly anchored, and with thumb and hind feet, it clutches her fur, hanging on for dear life. The mother then spends up to an hour getting to know her newborn. She licks it all over, then sniffs it to learn its scent.

Megabats are born wide awake, with thick hair and open eyes. Most microbat pups are born pink-skinned and hairless, with eyes closed. Their eyes open after a week to ten days. The pup nurses at least twice a day from one of two nipples found under the mother's wings.

Fruit-eating bat mothers carry their pups with them when they leave the roost to search for food. Insectivorous mothers, including Mexican free-tails, usually leave their young clinging to the cave ceiling. Some species form dense "baby clusters" that help them to keep warm. Millions of pups, up to five hundred per square foot, huddle together, covering the walls like a furry quilt. Squeaks, chirps, and cries echo throughout the cave, and the strong, sharp odor of ammonia from bat droppings fills the air.

Each mother returning to the roost searches for her own baby. How does she find her own hungry infant among the thousands of others in the colony? First, she can usually remember the area where she left it. She flies to that area and calls to her pup. She listens for its special chirping cry. Recognizing her baby's voice, she sniffs it for its familiar scent. Satisfied that this is indeed her pup, she licks its face and lips. The infant nestles under her wing and resumes nursing. Most microbat mothers nurse their newborn for one to two months. Large bats, such as flying foxes, may nurse for as long as five months.

After about two weeks, most microbat pups will hang beside their mothers. They begin to exercise their wings, spreading and flexing them. After four or five weeks, they make a few practice flights to the mouth of the cave to prepare for their first flight in their new world.

Left: *A Mexican free-tail mother finds her young among the many others in the cave.* Above: *A Gambian epauletted bat mother licking her pup*

A rat snake eating a Southeastern bat (Myotis eustroriparius)

BATS IN DANGER

Even though bats are excellent fliers, they must be ever-alert for **predators**, animals that hunt them. Red-tailed hawks may swoop down from the skies, twist and dart into a flock, and snatch a bat in flight. Great horned owls may lurk outside a cave or mine entrance ready to pounce on unsuspecting bats as they emerge to search for their nighttime meal. Barn owls keep an eye open for the small, furry creatures who trespass on their shadowy roosts. Rat snakes slither up to the roof of a cave to capture a bat for dinner. Raccoons and foxes, too, enjoy a juicy bat snack.

But of all the enemies that kill bats, the most dangerous are humans. Humans, victims of wrong ideas about bats, have been killing them by the millions.

The truth is that bats are much more helpful than they are harmful. They help to control crop pests and other insects that spread disease to humans and livestock. Think how many more harmful and destructive insects there would be if insectivorous bats were not here to eat tons of insect pests each night to keep down the insect population. Bats are needed in large numbers to help maintain the balance of nature.

Bats eat fruit, but they also help new fruit trees to grow.

Bats perform another important service to humanity in preserving the rain forests of our world. Our rain forests are in grave danger because developers are cutting them down at an alarming rate. Ecologists warn that if we continue to cut down our forests, we will destroy the earth's ecological system. Bats, along with birds and other animals, are nature's seeders. They play a vital part in helping to reforest our woodlands by spreading seeds of forest trees, shrubs, and plants. Bats also disperse the seeds or pollinate the flowers of trees that give us cashew nuts and cloves.

Most fruit-eating bats cannot digest seeds from their food. So seeds from their droppings land in clearings and sprout, and new trees spring up. If you enjoy eating avocados, bananas, mangoes, or figs, you may thank the fruit-eating bats of the world.

Nectivorous bats that pollinate cactus flowers help to maintain the ecosystem of the desert. Spreading seeds and pollen helps plants to produce seeds that grow into new plants. Many other small animals, birds, and insects depend on these plants for food, moisture, and shelter. If bats disappear, some plants, and the wildlife that depends on them, could disappear as well.

Harvesting bat guano in a cave in Thailand

Since farmers first began growing crops many centuries ago, they have known that bat **guano** (GWAHN-oh), or droppings, provides excellent fertilizer. Nowadays, mining guano in bat caves is less common because inexpensive fertilizer is widely available, but many people around the world still use guano to nourish the soil.

Biologists continue to study bats to discover how some of their special abilities work so they may use this knowledge to help people. For example, understanding how bats are able to echolocate has helped scientists to develop sonic head-gear, such as electronic echolocators, which helps people who can't see well to walk confidently. Because bats' brains and humans' brains are much the same, scientists hope to discover how our brains process sensory information by studying how bats' brains process sound.

There is still much to be learned about bat behavior that could help us to understand more about our universe. Unfortunately, through ignorance or superstition, many people have long mistaken bats for pests. They have exterminated them with poison, pesticides, and guns, and burned, smoked, or blasted them out of caves and mines. Chemicals and pesticides are still a serious threat to the survival of the bat population.

The building of new roads and highways, businesses and housing has destroyed many bat roosts. Caves and mines are often sealed shut to keep bats out, thereby destroying more of their homes.

You might think that with billions of bats in the world, there is little danger that they will become **extinct,** or die out until no more are left. But the threat of extinction is very real. Though bats are the longest-lived mammals of their size, they are the slowest to replace themselves because most give birth to only one pup a year. Most bats do not have offspring until they are two to two and one-half years old, and two-thirds of the bat population's offspring die during the first year. These small, fragile creatures may fall to their death inside the cave, fail to learn how to survive in the outside world, be eaten by predators, or be killed by people who mistakenly fear them. It takes time to replace entire colonies of perhaps millions of bats that humans have destroyed at one swoop. Many bat species are already extinct. Others are on the verge of disappearing. Almost 40 percent of bat species in the United States are on government lists of endangered species.

Indiana bats (Myotis sodalis), *like many other bats worldwide, are at risk of becoming extinct.*

Many people are trying to protect bats, such as these Mexican free-tails, and the caves where they roost.

What is being done to deal with this problem? The federal government now carries out environmental studies to avoid further destruction of these keepers of our ecology. Professional spelunkers, or cave explorers, are helping to save bats. They find and survey bat populations and help conservationists protect them.

Wildlife officials install heavy grates or fences across the entrances to important bat caves. They post warning signs at other caves to keep people from disturbing the bat residents. Some caves are protected by an alarm system that alerts officials when anyone enters a cave. Finally, recovery teams are carrying out plans to protect endangered bat species and start new colonies. But there is still much to be done.

What can you do?

Read and learn all you can about bats. Then you can tell people who say "ugh!" to bats that they are our friends, not our enemies. Tell others the facts about bats to dispel misinformation, myths, and superstitions. Let people know about the good that bats do. Encourage others not to destroy bats or their habitats. If you explore a cave or mine, do not disturb the bats. If you see a bat lying about, don't pick it up. It is probably ill or injured and may bite in self-defense. You can also join a bat conservation organization and volunteer to take part in conservation projects.

These lesser long-nosed bats are appealing, but like any wild animal, they should be left alone.

Bats do not make good pets because they are delicate creatures, easily injured. Their food, water, and temperature requirements are very specific, and caring for them takes a lot of time. But you may want to build a backyard bat house for these furry fliers. Bat watching is great fun. In the evening just at dusk, if you stand outdoors and watch closely, you may be lucky enough to see, silhouetted against the twilight sky, a colony of these friendly fliers of the night winging their way toward you.

GLOSSARY

adapt: to adjust or change to survive in an environment

colonies: groups of animals, such as bats, that live together for part or all of their lives

echolocation: a way of locating objects through the use of echoes

extinct: having no members of a species left alive

guano: the excrement of bats

gestation: the period of time between the fertilization of an egg and the birth of young

hibernate: to spend the winter in a sleeplike state

insectivorous: having a diet consisting of insects

mammals: animals that give birth to live young and nourish their young with milk from the mother's body

membrane: a thin layer of skin tissue

migrate: to move from one region to settle in another

nectivorous: having a diet consisting of plant nectar

nocturnal: active at night

ovulate: to produce an egg ready for fertilizing

predators: animals that kill and eat other animals

sonar: a way of using sound to detect objects

torpor: a sleeplike state in which the body's functions slow down considerably

ultrasonic: beyond the range of human hearing

uterus: a hollow organ in a female mammal's body

LEARN MORE ABOUT BATS

State agencies and private groups such as the National Audubon Society, Nature Conservancy, and spelunker organizations work hard on conservation. Bat Conservation International (BCI), founded in 1975 by Dr. Merlin Tuttle, is dedicated to the preservation and protection of bat populations. BCI has more than 12,000 members worldwide. If you would like to join them, write to:

> Bat Conservation International
> Box 162603
> Austin, TX 78716

INDEX

ABOUT THE AUTHOR

A full-time writer and the author of numerous books for adults, **Dee Stuart** has always been fascinated by animals. After writing *The Astonishing Armadillo,* her first book for children, she turned her attention to the intriguing and often misunderstood world of bats. Ms. Stuart and her husband have two children and three grandchildren. They live in Richardson, Texas.